28 Years
Since My Last Confession

28 Years

Since My Last Confession

Selected Poems

Catherine Powers

iUniverse LLC
Bloomington

28 YEARS SINCE MY LAST CONFESSION
Selected Poems

iUniverse books may be ordered through booksellers or by contacting:

iUniverse LLC
1663 Liberty Drive
Bloomington, IN 47403
www.iuniverse.com
1-800-Authors (1-800-288-4677)

ISBN: 978-1-4917-0445-5 (sc)
ISBN: 978-1-4917-0446-2 (e)

Library of Congress Control Number: 2013919166

Printed in the United States of America.

iUniverse rev. date: 10/31/2013

This book includes the following previously published poems and short stories: "Darts," published in a journal for the National Association of Social Workers, Michigan Chapter (2011); the short story "Beer Garden," published online in the Metro Times (2001); and the poems "I Learn Lessons," "As Life Would Have It," and "A Catalogue of Good-Byes," published by Northern Spies (1995).

Cover Photograph: The Powers family circa 1964 on Easter Sunday in front of my maternal grandmother's home at 33 Bright Street, Northampton, MA.

For every writer who has struggled to bring forth
a voice and let that voice loose in the world

Acknowledgments

I am profoundly grateful and owe my deepest thanks to the following people:

My friends Christie Urgo de Lozano and Dorothy Ruelle Elliott. Christie, you were celebrating this book long before it was written. Dorothy, you have always believed in my abilities even when I didn't. A woman is lucky to have one such friend in her life, and I have two.

My friend Lisa Lane, writer and screenwriter. Our weekly telephone calls have meant the world to me. When I felt that the tasks ahead were overwhelming and that this book would never happen, your advice, insights, and good cheer kept me moving forward. I can't wait to see your name in the film credits.

My friend Mike Fedel, an extraordinary writer and poet as well as a fantastic blog partner (www.annarborpoetsonline.blogspot.com).

My high school English teacher, Mary Jo Crane, who sent my writing to the Scholastic Art & Writing Awards and who treated a messed up seventeen-year-old with loving kindness. I held on to that award through many a dark hour (and I'm not being dramatic here). You are the best.

My two teachers and friends Jim Johnston and Kay Gould-Caskey, writers themselves and owners of Falling Water Books & Collectibles and the Center for Creative Pursuits. Twenty years ago you both helped me find my voice, and you have encouraged and supported me ever since. In a world that loves a critic, your noncritical teaching and feedback allows writers to dive deep and write from the heart.

My friend the poet Karen Totten. Thank you for your ongoing encouragement and last-minute editorial advice.

My friend the actress, painter, and hair stylist, the incomparable Sinderella (Cynthia Herrmann). You are a steady source of inspiration for what it means to be an artist in the world.

Vijaya Ramesh, MD. Your down-to-earth approach to navigating the storms of life has helped me again and again.

Kathy Reilly, PhD. Kathy, I can't thank you enough for being the brave, intuitive, and brilliant psychologist that you are.

Lori Perpich, MA. Lori, I have counted on your common-sense intelligence, compassion, and humor. You have never let me down. My writing group at the Center for Creative Pursuits. Your talent and creativity continue to inspire me week after week. I feel privileged to be among you all.

ARTS Anonymous.

Lastly, I wish to thank Walter Powers. You are a true partner and my personal cheering squad. I rely on your insights and instincts. Thanks for sticking with me. Here's to another twenty years of adventure!

Contents

I Learn Lessons

The day itches like dead skin
Some fungus crawling around
I would prefer higher forms of life
But I'm practicing acceptance

Crawl

Eat fear
I guess at what this means
I think of this often

Digestion

At a carnival once
A leather woman with a rat tease
Had a tattoo:
Sworn to Fun, Loyal to None

I can relate

TLA
That stands for True Love Always
It was carved over and over
On every bathroom door of my high school
So much love then!

Love

Darts

My alcoholic brother
Was a master of darts
Bar darts in particular
Even while his voice would slur
And his six-foot-five body would sway
(like a tall building during heavy winds)
He could still get that good eye going
Take what remained of his concentration and focus
Pour it into a pint glass
And . . .

Game On!
Three in a Bed
Two Fat Ladies
Diddle for the Middle
Right Church, Wrong Pew
The words and phrases
Tumbling out cool and clean
Nary a mumble
All clear
In the corner pocket

How do I know this?
A half hour before
I'd get that boozed-up call
Begging for a ride home—
He'd walked to the bar hours earlier
Only two sheets to the wind then
"Could you do me a *huge* favor?"
The word *huge* dragged out
Like he'd been practicing on it all day

I'd enter whatever bar he graced that night
Where he'd commence with the pleading
Two more minutes
Two more minutes
Just two more minutes, please
The game at a critical juncture
So I'd sit down in the chair
And wait

And wait
Wait

Finally I'd head to the door
Yell back to him
"You're the one who called me!"
He'd hear me then
Pour his last beer into a to-go cup
That he'd always carry with him
Like a talisman or a rabbit's foot or any good-luck charm
Him weaving and smiling
We'd make our way to the car

"I owe you one," he'd say
"You owe me about fifteen," I'd counter
"Ha!" he would bellow
Excited, eyes tearing
"No, no, I really owe you one"
Then he'd turn his face
Shift his body toward the passenger door
Be asleep before I could tell him
This is really the last time
Really, really
Really the last time

For my brother, Bill Powers, who died sober at age forty-nine

As Life Would Have It

After six years
We fell madly in doubt
I opened the window
We both climbed out

God Is Tired

The family is sick and miserable
Or failing a grade
Or experiencing a nervous condition
We say we're praying for things to get better
But that's not true
No one has said a single prayer
Or lit a candle
The last time I got down on my knees
Was to look for change under the bed
God sees through this poor-ass charade
We're not putting anything over on Him
From the looks of things
I'd say he's tired of the bullshit

Please Go

I'd give you a penny
I'd give you a pound
I'd give all my Christmas Club money
Not to have you around

Mid-New England Small-Town Amusement Park

As wide and as long as two city blocks
Limited selection of rides and amusements
The Whirl, Dinosaur Fun House
A small carousel with two damaged horses
Space Ring, Animal Land
Populated by fiberglass animals—a wondrous space-age material
And one lone dinosaur who must have escaped from the fun house
Crash Carts
Ride all day
One dollar and fifty cents
No height requirements
No Must Be Accompanied by an Adult
One entire summer
My father would drop us off at noon
His four kids ages five, seven, nine, and eleven
Me eleven then
Pick us up a half hour before the park would close

Whatever he did without us
It was worth the six dollars
This for a man
So tightfisted
He believed children
Should buy their own toys

The trip home at sunset
Better than the park for me
No babysitting that rambunctious brood
Staring out the rear window
The night dark and warm
Lying on the car's backseat
I'm the only kid awake
Hypnotized by the stars brightening
Then darkening
And the electric wires
Counting, counting, counting
Everything passing by so quickly

A Catalogue of Good-byes

I dream
Zippered
Hungry
Holding my breath
Losing time like money
The edgy moon too tight
Your handprint on my thigh
I will be forty-one in the year 2000
But I am still young
My mother says

My mother says

You Are to Me Like the Plague

I avoid you like the plague
Although I have never had the plague
Or known anyone with the plague
So I can't say for sure that I avoid you in this manner

Truth be told then
I avoid you more than I avoid the plague
I already wash my hands—what? Ten times a day?
From knowledge I've gleaned
From dishwashing commercials and
Kitchen cleaning product commercials
There are viruses and bacteria and super-organisms of a distinctly
    untoward nature
That live among us (me) and wait like a hopeful suitor
To invade our systems (mine)
And lay waste to all that we (I) hold dear

So the plague is not big enough for how much I do not want to
    see you
Or hear of you
Or speak your name
Or read about you third-hand
From another woman
Who just has to share
How delightful it was to meet you
"Finally, a man who actually *reads!*"
"And *writes* too!"
Uh, right
"It was delightful to meet you!"
It always was—he was great at meeting
"I hope to see you again soon!"

I read once that early plague symptoms include

- buboes (enlarged lymph nodes under the armpits, in the neck or in the groin)
- severe headache
- vomiting
- decreased appetite
- abdominal pain
- diarrhea—which may be bloody

I had five out of six of these symptoms
The buboes I chalk up to too much fast-food takeout
But you could have caused them too
I'll give you that much power
I suppose I should be grateful I never experienced

- delirium and death

In closing
I will cross the street if I see you
I will ask a mutual friend to change the subject
If your name comes up
I will delete every e-mail that you sent to me
And every "love" note written on blank, ripped-out pages from my
    journal
This is my antibiotic
This is my partial cure
I wish I could warn others
But I'm not sure they'd believe me
If you've never had the plague
It's hard to believe it really exists

Catholics and Jehovah's

We're Catholic
I tell the Jehovah's Witness girl two houses over
Everybody knows her family
They try to sell the neighborhood
Magazines nobody wants to buy

Yesterday the Jehovah's Witness girl told me
You're going to hell
You and your family
You see God's only invited a certain number to heaven
And they're all Jehovah's

How many? I ask
The number she's gotten
Is one hundred and forty-four thousand newly cleansed souls
I don't even know how much that is yet
But it sounds like there's still plenty of room

When I tell my mother this
She tells me not to believe a goddamn thing
Anyone in that family tells me
They're still upset
Because your BB-gun-happy brother
Shot their kid in the head
And the cops backed me up because
They're all friends with your grandfather

Furthermore
That's not a religion that makes any sense
If it did
Why would they be pounding on our door and
Trying to sell it to us like it was a Hoover?

Mother Poem

In a dream
You were an actress
You had the starring role
After the play I ran backstage
You looked at me, shrugged
Did not remember me as your child
The play had a name
Not Now, Not Ever
It is your big break

Leg

Ma watches the man push the power mower
Up the steep incline that is his yard
The man strains the system that is his body
Pushing self and machine
At a dangerous angle
"That man is going to lose a leg," she says
"Whether he wants to or not"

What We Are Telling People

As far as anyone knows
You're a nice normal girl
You'd fool people into believing it
If you'd stop being so dramatic
Susan Hayward headed to the gas chamber
Greta Garbo dying of consumption
You're too much like a fire hose
A lot of pressure and force
You'd no doubt find life calmer
Happier and more predictable
If you could learn to point that hose in the right direction

None Too Far Away

I.
My grandmother's mother
Took with her from Ireland
A mahogany chest
A lock of her dead sister's hair and
A tintype of my great-grandfather
Killed in the Boer Wars

They also brought with them melancholy
It came over on the boat
In addition they transported distrust
For reaching beyond one's means or station
My people
A genetic pool of tall, red-haired
Angry, violent potato eaters
Descended from Viking relations
That raped and plundered
Villages and small towns
DNA for swollen lips and black eyes
The history is everyone split up
Not long after they reached shore
They hadn't seen the sun for weeks
Or months or years
It gave them just enough
A loose thread of hope
There might be more to life than fighting

II.
Me?
I just hold in my wings
Hoping someone will notice
I do not have children
The plan is to keep my hands on the keyboard
Busy and out of the devil's way
I am to tell their stories

Postcard Found while Walking Dog

Grandpa is dying in the attic
Everyone screams at everyone else
The worst ones are Cousin Becky
And Grandma Nestor

The only good thing is
The landlord has asked us to move out
All the yelling and noise
Is getting on the neighborhood's nerves
Plus he doesn't want the city visiting
And making him fix the lead
We don't know where we're going
But Cousin Becky says the government's got to help us

Wish you were here
Love, Eric

PS We all got head lice from Ricky's hat

Personnel

I can't decide on a career
My father suggests
I would be good in personnel
My father left the personnel department
At the VA Hospital ten years ago
He now regrets this choice
Especially when he finds out his old job
Pays twice as much as he makes now
With benefits

"What do you do in personnel?" I ask
He tells me that you hire and fire people
"Anything else?"
"Well, you read them their rights"

I don't know why he thinks I'd be good at that

Another Thing

You need to get over it
My mother told me
What?
Your childhood
My entire childhood?
No, just all those memories
That make you so depressed and upset
What memories? I ask
Everything that I ever told you
That made me upset
Or traumatized me
Or just made me sad
You claim never happened
So what is it exactly
I have to get over?

Trash Night

Ma is on a cleaning bender
Since the divorce she's gotten nuttier
Our three-bedroom ranch home
Must be purged of all trash and garbage
Inside and out

The trash can't sit at the back of the garage
Not even for two days
Its presence so close to the clean house
Risks contamination of the entire system
Unseen spawn generate
Reproduce at an alarming rate
Germinate and hatch
Find their way back into the clean house
Don't look at her that way
It happens

And while the night seethes blue and black
Ma drives the surrounding streets
Hooded and determined
Her two boys in the front seat
Her two girls in the back
The plastic bagged trash
Stinking and straining against
The side windows and the rear window hatch

"Come on, come on"
She slaps the steering wheel
It is 3:00 a.m.
The hours tick down till the start of the school day
We'll keep searching until we find a neighborhood that will take us
Where our refuse can be placed
Where our debris will blend easily
Alongside the garbage of good sleeping folks

It's only a matter of time now

It has to be trash night somewhere

Genetics from My Grandmother On

I'm a mix of your daughter
And her husband
My father
Nothing came through those two
That was ever straight or clear
But that's genetics for you
Peas
A petri dish
Dominant and recessive
All I can tell you is
From my knowledge of science
I had
Absolutely
Irrefutably
No say
In any of it

It All Comes Out

Why is it poetry if the red heron speaks?
Is it the juxtaposition?
It would have to be wouldn't it?
It couldn't be the verbs
Where's the lovely in *is?*
Where's the charm or astonishment in *speak?*

What about the good pit bull?
Just the word *pit bull*
Voiced in most contexts
Notice how your breath stops
Your heart beats faster
For most of us anyway
The exception being pit bulls
Pit bull owners and animal shelter workers
Even in a joke
"Two pit bulls walk into a bar . . ."
You sense this one will not end happily

On my street each weekday morning
A mother walks with her young son
Every day she is fifteen minutes late
She holds his hand tightly
She is small and round like a blueberry
Her son is earnest and accommodating
I don't know their story
But I give them a new one every week
It's gotten so I don't bother to turn on morning TV
Until they're beyond my horizon

Just this morning
After months of this
It occurred to me that maybe that boy
Isn't going to school
And further
He may not be a boy
He may be a very boyish girl
And his mother?
She may not be his mother

I heard God in that moment
He told me
"That's what you get for assumptions"
I nodded
Thought back to God
You're right

Later, in the shower
I began to think
What do I get with assumptions?
I mean don't you have to have a couple thousand
Just to get out of bed
Brush your teeth
Comb your hair
Feed the bird
Why work if you can't assume
Come Friday you'll get a paycheck
To pay for the gas to get you to work
To buy the carry-out sandwich
Because you were too tired to make food the night before

One time I assumed the ice on Orr Lake was frozen
To test this assumption I stomped my foot as hard as I could
The ice cracked
I went down
Water up to my waist
My snowsuit an anchor
As the local newspaper reported
I'm lucky to be alive

In retrospect I decided
That was a fucked-up thing for God to say
Who needs the mind games?
The one-upmanship
I'm just a woman who's trying to get along

Still
I thank you for listening
You've all been incredibly patient
It's not everyone
That can tolerate whatever it is I've got going on

Therapy

When my therapist left the room
I took a look at the notes she had written
There was nothing on the page for our session
Except the phrase scribbled too large in black ink
In handwriting that could only be described as disappointed
"No fresh insights"

Twenty-Eight Years since
My Last Confession

If Christ sat next to you in a college class and wanted to borrow
    your notes
Even though he had not attended one single class
Would you let him?

Or if he wanted you to cosign a loan
For a sports car with a moon roof and a spoiler
Would you place your signature beside his
On the black dotted line?

If he wore too much of a cologne you found offensive
Talked loudly in movie theaters
Voted Republican
Fed his kids too much sugar and fast food
Could you love him as a friend and
Not as a savior?

Note from My Angry Boss Two
Days before He Fires Me

I know you're trying to write a novel or something
I can respect that
I wanted to be a fireman when I was in second grade
Everybody has a dream
I know I said you could work on your "projects" during downtime
My question is this
Have you done any goddamn work this week?
Any?

A Highly Entertaining
Total Waste of Time

He takes Klonopin
He told me this right off
His last girlfriend was pulled over in Arizona
It was her fourth DUI
Rather than paying the two grand it would take for bail
She told the judge to give her the thirty days
He said that she's *that* tough
There seemed to be an ache in his voice when he told me that
She's that tough
But the bad thing he said
Is that he's just too old for this
Besides her being twenty years younger
She packed a hell of a punch
She broke his nose and messed up his right eye
And what could he do?
He didn't hit her back
It was hormones
Or probably hormones
Or the hormones and the list of things that she kept
Bottled up inside until they exploded
Oh! And
They had kids the same age which was nice
They all loved the zoo

When it got quiet
I told him well at least you haven't set the bar
Too high for dating

He'd been a respected artist once
Sold stuff like Arts and Crafts doors for ten thousand dollars
Rich people paid that kind of ridiculous money
Ass pains though
Real ass pains he said
You jacked up the price every time with Richie Rich
You built the ass pain into the price
Because it would never be easy with them

He bought dinner and he dressed well
He didn't try to maul me or force his tongue down my throat
When I thanked him for driving an hour for our date
He told me it was better
Than sitting home watching *CSI Miami*
I told him I wish I had a dollar
For every time I had heard that from a guy!

When I get home I try to put the night into perspective
So I don't get depressed and think this is it
This is what you get for
Divorcing a man who loved you
Who loves you still
Who still tells all his friends
Including my mother
That we are soulmates
We always will be

It was just a date
A sizing up
Don't make it bigger than it was
Don't make it into a metaphor
Four hours does not a lifetime make

Just hope he doesn't call back

Or if he does
Use your Irish diplomacy
Tell him he is way too much man for you
That your creative differences
Are just too immense
He won't buy it
But that's not your problem
He will appreciate your
Good-natured attempt at humor

The World the Way She Wanted It

My mother changed the rules for her benefit
Besides, she never thought of them as rules anyway
In drawn-out arguments
Business or personal
She would end them by saying,
"Let's compromise here—
Do it my way this time"
Except later you'd realize
You never had a next time

When bowling she didn't adhere to the ten-frame rule
That type of structure messed up what could be a perfect game
So while others kept their strikes and spares
Etched with a tiny pencil stub onto a small sheet of paper
She bowled on and on
Until she felt her final score
Matched the number in her head
If you tried to reason with her
She'd just head off to the snack bar

I've tried to emulate
Her attitude of entitlement but
It takes a panache and an obliviousness
I do not possess
The closest I've ever come
Is getting a salesman
To lower the retail price by 10 percent
On a couch or a chair

Which I now realize
Everyone can get
Just by the asking

Pie: A Metaphor

You split
I pick—
The method that was meant to ensure
Fairness and uniformity and
To guard against the greed and ruthless capitalism
That drove certain family members

Never Enough

The answer to how many cookies are left in the jar
The answer to how much ice cream is left in the carton
The economic question underlying it all:
How much?
The correct answer in my family:
Enough to fight over

Apples

My aunt was married to an apple farmer
She'd been twice divorced by the time she met him
Most of her problems
Were because she got involved with men
Who didn't like to work
Or stopped working soon after she married them

My brother always had to pick fights
With her apple farmer husband
At family gatherings
After a few drinks he'd start blaming Ben
For all the apple problems in the world
What had happened to the apples he ate as a boy?
You used to be able to count on Empires at least
Now everything was genetically modified
Ben insisted he had no hand in this
No one up his way was modifying anything
It was mid-Michigan after all

There was no leaving it alone
With my brother though
He would not be satisfied
Until all the relatives took a side
He lived to divide people up
Make them feel defensive
And for absolutely no reason—guilty

As I got older I realized
Conflict was my brother's daily vitamin
He swallowed it dry
Never to lodge in his throat
The apples only an excuse

My Brother's Depression

It lasted almost a year
Then obsessions took over
The strangest being a penchant
For searching the Internet
For photos of celebrities when they were young and famous
And then finding photos of them now
When they are not

Broke

My heart didn't break
But a lot of me broke
I remember as a kid
Learning about Mrs. Duffan
Our neighbor three doors down
Who had a nervous breakdown

I imagined she was going along just fine
Slightly nervous or very nervous
Then a bad thing happened
Her husband a secret cheat
Maybe her baby died before he was born
Or the horse track ate up life savings
Then years of accumulated sadness
Finally broke her mind in two

There are different words for this
Words that claim to be more exact
To the psychological process that occurs
But I tell you
If you have not been there
Broke is the operative word
You stop
You don't continue
Offered a huge sum
To cook, to clean, to study, to work
To be the creature you were the year before
Or five years before
To maintain this woman for a week or two weeks
You would not be able to accept the money

You will try to be that old you
She could at least fake it
But that avenue is closed
Like a crime scene
With invisible crime scene tape
And the crime happened inside you

Nervous doesn't apply here
You are the car dead by the side of the road
Who knows if it can be repaired?
It is all broke things and more
A breakdown

This is it:
It is the crack in the ceiling
That keeps getting bigger
Maybe you caused it
Because you didn't patch it
While you still had a chance
Or maybe it was always there just
Hiding under the plaster
Whatever
It is what it is
And what it is
Is broke

Free Advice from My Mother

It's as easy to marry a rich man as a poor man
Don't worry about smoking
By the time you get cancer
They'll have developed a cure

Insurance is meant to be used
Why bother paying all those premiums
If you can't use it once in a while
Put in a claim for repairs
Just remember to read the policy carefully
To know beforehand what will be covered
Don't forget your agent at Christmas
Even if it's just a fruitcake or a calendar
You'll kick yourself if you go cheap
And later get denied full compensation

Nobody likes complainers
Or the boo hoo hoo
I can't get over my childhood types
If you've got a problem talk to the priest
He has to keep your confessional secrets
While psychiatrists will write down
All your personal skeletons
Then charge you big money
For what you should have known in the first place
Keep your problems to yourself
It will help build your character

Free Advice from My Siblings

It never really happened
We don't remember that and
It certainly didn't happen *that* way
Even if it did
Why bring it up now?
You live too much in the past
Not a happy past either
Try living in the present for a change
Nine out of ten recommend it
Besides your father was a war hero and
Your mother is prone to hyperventilation
They don't need this
Not at their age
Can't you just put this drama on hold
For a few more years?
Maybe you'll forget your troubles
Or if you can't or won't
By then they'll be gone and
You'll only ruin a dead person's reputation
Which is a lot better than a live person
Which is what you're contemplating now

Sand

I needed a permit to toss your ashes into the ocean
They're considered human remains (which they are)
Or cremains (which hardly makes it as a euphemism)
So instead I tipped you into a plastic pail
Mixed you with an equal amount of sand
Turned you onto the beach
Made our last castle together
And watched you wash out to sea

Snow

Easy to trust its cold brightness
Over which you have no control

TARDIS

My ex-husband told me about Time Lords
The great time/space engine left behind
Disguised as an innocent phone booth
That when you entered a TARDIS
You stepped out of your reality and into another
So many unexplained phenomena
Mysteries that only the select Lords are privy to
Sadly in the case of our marriage
We never stumbled upon this machine
Or if we did
We never recognized it
Leaving us sadly in a dimensional loop where
We could only leave by ending it

Yellow

A color I never wear
Too alive
Too jump-off-the-page
A walking race stripe
A bowl of lemons
A huge dose of sun
A smiley-face sticker
On a ten-year-old's backpack
Have a Happy Day!
A color God invented
As he pondered an eight-day week
Then thought better

Profile

If I had nothing to compare my life to
I might have been happy
If I had been hatched
Instead of brought up
I might have avoided lengthy suffering
Or maybe sorrow
(Suffering is what I cultivated from sorrow)
If I had not watched afternoon movies as a child
Read books
Looked at night into our neighbors' picture windows
Things might have worked out

"The secret to happiness
Is to hold very low expectations"
I don't know where I first heard this
When I was younger I found it a cynical contemptuous statement
By my forties I'd lived into its accuracy
Its wisdom
Its simplicity and sophistication
I created a genuine gospel from the phrase
I write it in soap on car windows
And on bathroom mirrors
I share the phrase with coworkers
When they complain of long hours and low wages
Who look at me with awe or resentment
Who call me The Philosopher or
The Dali Lama's auburn-haired cousin

I sit in my bedroom
On the bed with no headboard
Propped up by five pillows
As straight and down-to-earth
As the letter *L*
I am not a starving African country
Or a well-pensioned traveler
Or a woman with a flat belly
If for one hour I stop the comparisons
I know for that space
I can be happy
I have that potential

Forgetting to Plan My Life

I saw a T-shirt with a word inscribed: PUSH
Pray Until Something Happens
It was there in a rack of shirts at Goodwill
Wedged in between breast cancer awareness runs
The reptiles of the Florida Everglades
And shirts promoting long-dead start-up companies
I'd like to think that was God slipping me a hint
Or at least a very obvious suggestion

Entrepreneur

These are the jobs I held as a child:

Papergirl
Seed seller
Babysitter
Curbside number painter
(Until the city cracked down—apparently I needed a vendor license)
Weed puller
Night crawler catcher
Bottle scavenger and bottle returner
Lilac and pussy willow floral artist
Spider killer
(I was the only person in my family not afraid of them and
received a nickel for every dead spider)

I worked for myself then
No boss
No deadlines
The cost of living minimal

Together

After Isabelle died
It became apparent
That the bed was no longer
The friendly and inviting place
It had been before

Some marriages are kept together for the children
But ours was kept together by the dog
Or for the dog
As we knew she would never understand
Where the other one went
We could not explain it to her
In a way that she would comprehend
You tried once
We separated for eleven days
You moved to your mother's home
While I attempted to divert amuse and distract
The inconsolable shepherd
For hours every day
She would wander back and forth in front of the living-room
    window
Each broken muffler on an ancient Honda Civic
Elicited such anticipation
That I had to call you
Summon you to come back
Her grief too great
Unfathomable
Profound in a cavernous way
The pack needed its collective
The pack had to stay together

A month after we buried her in the backyard
When it was still both our home
The bed became the corner
To share our mutual grief
We knew that soon would come the time
The one Isabelle had forestalled
Not today though
We said
Not today

Mistake

I like to think of you as a brief, horrible mistake
A miserable slip-up
A calculation gone wrong
A renter whom I welcomed into my home
(Home being a metaphor for my body)
Whose references checked out
(I took those references at face value)
Only to learn later
You received such glowing accounts
Because no one knew how
To free themselves from your clutches
Except to pass you on to me

The Blood of Jesus

Whatever sin enslaves me
The blood of Jesus Christ
Can set me free
Whatever temptation has me bound
The blood of my Lord
Can untie the rope

Beside the highway three white crosses
Follow me from Kentucky to Tennessee
Reminding me of the blood he shed
Walking the road to Calvary
Then there's the thorn crown
The sadistic guards
The awful jeering crowds
So much blood and violence in his story
For a peaceful man
A man who worked with wood and his hands

I don't want to believe he died for me
If I stood in the garden at Gethsemane
I would have crossed God
Tell him it was so unnecessary
Would set a bad precedent
Would remove the joy in the life he'd led
Bring a spring and summer of sadness
A fall and winter of grief
I'd ask them all
Father, Son, Holy Spirit
To reconsider this end
To rewrite this history
Would it be so tragic
Ruin everything
To have God die with a smile
In his bed comforted
Grateful to all who loved him

Payout

If I could send you packing
I would
The mediator won't let me
We've got to be reasonable
Or we're going to lose everything to the lawyers
So this is what I propose
Since compromise isn't our strong suit
We start flipping coins
Or rolling dice
To settle who gets the bed
Who ends up with the sofa
The way I see us is
We were like an unhappy slot machine
The one in the corner with all the flash and the noise
Play Day or Dream Lover
Or Work No More or Ship Comes In
The one that would almost hit big
And only pay out occasionally
So we kept stuffing it with quarters
Telling ourselves we'd spent too much
To leave and go home

The Gap

The crack where God slips in
Where light enters
Where hope finds a toehold
A chink in the personal armor
Where that which is broken
Is the channel
That allows the healing to begin